**HEINEMANN STATE STUDIES**

# All Around
# Virginia
## Regions and Resources

Karla Smith

**Heinemann Library**
Chicago, Illinois

© 2003 Heinemann Library
a division of Reed Elsevier Inc.
Chicago, Illinois

Customer Service  888-454-2279

Visit our website at www.heinemannlibrary.com

Designed by Heinemann Library
Page layout by Wilkinson Design
Printed and bound in the United States by Lake Book Manufacturing, Inc.

07 06 05 04 03
10 9 8 7 6 5 4 3 2 1

**Library of Congress
Cataloging-in-Publication Data**

Smith, Karla, 1947-
    All around Virginia : regions and resources / Karla Smith.
        p. cm. --  (Heinemann state studies)
    Summary: Provides an overview of the state of Virginia, includ-
    ing discussion of the various regions, how each is different, and
        what each contributes to the state and its people.
    Includes bibliographical references and index.
    ISBN 1-4034-0358-9 -- ISBN 1-4034-0580-8 (pbk.)
    1. Virginia--Geography--Juvenile literature.  2. Regionalism
    --Virginia--Juvenile literature.   [1. Virginia--Geography.]
    I. Title. II. Series.
    F226.3.S65 2003
    917.55--dc21

                                    2002152949

**Acknowledgments**

The author and publishers are grateful to the following for permission to reproduce copyright material:

Cover photographs by Everett Johnson/Index Stock Imagery, (L-R) James L. Amos/Corbis, Alex Brandon/Heinemann Library, Alex Brandon/Heinemann Library, Alex Brandon/Heinemann Library

Title page (L-R) David Hawkhurst/Chesapeake Bay Oyster Foundation, Alex Brandon/Heinemann Library, Janet Hitchen Photography; contents page Jeff Gnass; p. 9 Jeffrey Howe/Visuals Unlimited; p. 11 Jeff Greenberg/Visuals Unlimited; p. 13 J&L Waldman/Bruce Coleman, Inc.; p. 14 Lowell Georgia/Corbis; p. 15 Richmond Times Dispatch; p. 16 Adrin Snider/AP Wide World Photos; pp. 17, 22, 25, 30 Alex Brandon/Heinemann Library; p. 18 James L. Amos/Corbis; p. 19T David Hawkhurst/Chesapeake Bay Oyster Foundation; p. 19B Gary C. Knapp/AP Wide World Photos; p. 20T Gloucester-Mathews Gazette-Journal, Gloucester, VA; p. 21 Carl Purcell; p. 23 John Faber; p. 24 Holt Confer/The Image Works; p. 26 Janet Hitchen Photography; p. 27 Kenneth Garrett; p. 29 Jack Hollingsworth/Corbis; p. 31 Jeff Gnass; p. 35 Virginia Tourism Corp.; p. 37 Bob & Ann Simpson/Visuals Unlimited; p. 38 Jenny Hager/The Image Works; p. 40 Richard T. Nowitz; p. 41 Mae Scanlan; p. 42 Getty Images; p. 44 Steve Solum/Bruce Coleman, Inc.

Photo research by Julie Laffin

Special thanks to Gary Barr and Jean Hodges for their expert advice on the series.

Some words are shown in bold, **like this.**
You can find out what they mean by looking in the glossary.

# Contents

# Virginia's Geography and Resources

The variety of **physical** geography in Virginia makes it an interesting and attractive place. The Blue Ridge Mountains, some of the oldest mountains in North America, are in the west. There are sandy beaches in the east and coastal shorelines that run for 3,315 miles. In addition, there are almost 50,000 miles of freshwater rivers, plus numerous valleys, plains, hills, and forests.

Virginia has five key geographic regions. Each is defined by features such as mountains, hills, valleys, or plains. These regions are the Coastal Plain (or Tidewater), Piedmont, Blue Ridge Mountains, Valley and Ridge, and Appalachian **Plateau.**

Over seven million Virginians live in all these regions. They use each region's **natural resources** for **industry** and farming. **Human resources** are the people that create goods and services. People live in Virginia for many reasons, such as its beauty, location, and jobs. Transportation routes help move the products Virginians make to markets all over the world.

## LOCATION

Virginia covers over 400 miles of land from the Atlantic Ocean and Chesapeake Bay in the east to the Appalachian Mountains in the west. The Potomac River forms 180 miles of its northern boundary. The state is almost 200 miles from north to south.

## Virginia's Location and Regions

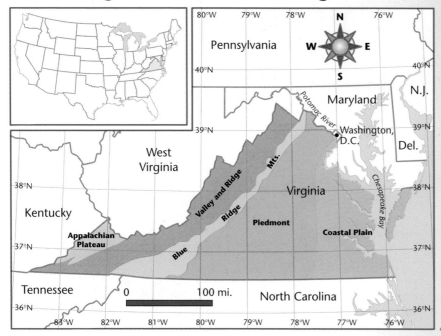

*Five states share Virginia's borders: Maryland, West Virginia, Kentucky, Tennessee, and North Carolina. Washington, D.C., the nation's capital, is to the northeast.*

Virginia is divided into 95 counties. The counties of northern and eastern Virginia are crowded and **urban.** Fairfax County is Virginia's most populated county, with more than 700,000 people. Many counties in Virginia are **rural.** Farms and forests fill the rural areas, and the towns are small.

Virginia's three largest cities by population are Virginia Beach, Norfolk, and Richmond. They are located in an area known as the **Urban Corridor.** Cities in the Urban Corridor stretch in a line from Arlington in northern Virginia to Virginia Beach in southeast Virginia.

**To find out more about Virginia's population, see the map on page 12.**

## USING RESOURCES

Natural resources are materials found in nature that can be used by people. Valuable natural resources in Virginia include forests, water, land, and **minerals.** Natural resources provide materials used to make things people use. This in turn creates jobs, since people are needed to make the goods out of the resources. Human

# Virginia Resources

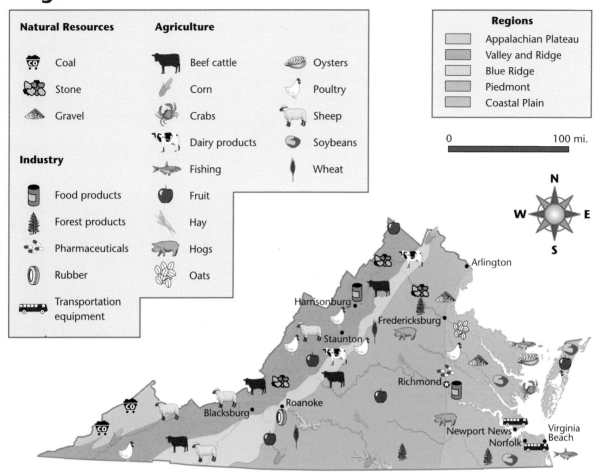

## Natural Resources

- Coal
- Stone
- Gravel

## Industry

- Food products
- Forest products
- Pharmaceuticals
- Rubber
- Transportation equipment

## Agriculture

- Beef cattle
- Corn
- Crabs
- Dairy products
- Fishing
- Fruit
- Hay
- Hogs
- Oats
- Oysters
- Poultry
- Sheep
- Soybeans
- Wheat

## Regions

- Appalachian Plateau
- Valley and Ridge
- Blue Ridge
- Piedmont
- Coastal Plain

0    100 mi.

N W E S

Arlington
Harrisonburg
Fredericksburg
Staunton
Richmond
Roanoke
Blacksburg
Newport News
Norfolk
Virginia Beach

*The map above shows some of the products found or made in Virginia. The state has a variety of natural resources, from which many different products are made.*

resources, also called labor, include all the people who work to make **natural resources** useful to people.

The rich and varied geography in Virginia means that each region has a variety of natural resources that help the **economy** of the state. For example, important **industries** such as fishing and shipbuilding are found along its shoreline, and its many rivers provide freshwater products and transportation routes. Its mountains and beaches draw many visitors, while its different **landforms** support numerous farming and forest products.

Forests are one of Virginia's most valuable natural resources. Forests cover two-thirds of Virginia's land area, or 16 million acres. Virginia's forest products are

# The Virginia Economy
## Its Natural, Capital, and Human Resources
### Gross State Product (in dollars)

|  |  |
|---|---|
| Services | $61.5 billion |
| Government | $46.2 billion |
| Financial Industries | $46 billion |
| Trade | $37 billion |
| Manufacturing | $31.8 billion |
| Transportation & Utilities | $23 billion |
| Construction | $12.5 billion |
| Agriculture, Forestry, Fishing | $2.3 billion |
| Mining | $1 billion |

**Total Gross State Product: $261.3 billion**

*Most recent information according to the U.S. Department of Commerce, Bureau of Economic Analysis, 2000

*The graph above shows which industries are most important to Virginia's economy. The industry that makes the most money for the state is the service industry.*

important to the state's economy. More than 248,000 jobs in the state are related to forest products. The forest industry includes sawmills, paper **manufacturing,** and furniture factories.

Each year, the forest industry adds around 11.5 billion dollars to Virginia's economy. In the last 50 years, enough lumber has been harvested from Virginia's forests to build more than six million homes. Most of Virginia's forests are second or third growth forests. This means that the land has been used for farming in the past. Hardwoods and pines are the main types of trees.

But forests are not only useful for their lumber. Lumber and paper companies own just 10 percent of the timberland. The rest is owned by private landowners and the government. Much of it has been made into parks, wilderness, and scenic or historic areas for people to enjoy. More than six million people visited Virginia's

# Virginia Precipitation

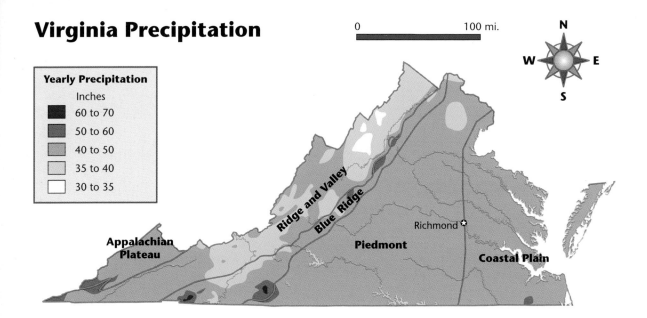

**Yearly Precipitation**
Inches
- 60 to 70
- 50 to 60
- 40 to 50
- 35 to 40
- 30 to 35

0          100 mi.

N
W    E
S

Ridge and Valley
Blue Ridge
Appalachian Plateau
Piedmont
Richmond
Coastal Plain

*Virginia has a mild climate and receives about 40 inches of rain each year. This makes it an ideal growing location for many types of crops.*

79,000 acres of forests in 2000. The money that tourists spent in in Virginia contributed to the state's **economy.**

Virginia's Seed Tree Law says that landowners in the state must replant new trees when timber is cut or harvested. This helps keep forests useful to the economy. Planting new trees helps keep the forest green and healthy. The loblolly pine is the most frequently planted tree.

Water is another important **natural resource** across the state. Rainfall provides water for streams, rivers, lakes, **reservoirs,** and **aquifers,** which provide people with

## Tourism

**Tourism** is one of Virginia's biggest businesses. Skiing in winter; hiking in the mountains; white-water rafting; and visiting caves, beaches, national and state parks, historic homes, and Civil War battlefields are just some of the things to do in Virginia. People use the artificial lakes of Virginia for **recreation,** too. Many state parks are located on their shores.

fresh water for drinking, bathing, and watering crops. Virginia's average annual rainfall is 42.8 inches, and its rivers flow with 25 billion gallons of water each day.

Virginia has only two natural lakes, Lake Drummond and Mountain Lake. But the state has 248 **artificial** lakes. Damming rivers and streams creates artificial lakes, which are used as reservoirs to store water and to make electricity. When the force of flowing water is used to produce electricity, it is called **hydroelectric** power. This is an example of how people change an environment to make living there easier. It is also an example of how people use natural resources.

Virginia's location, **climate,** and many natural resources make it an attractive place for people to live. Over seven million Virginians live and work in a wide variety of jobs in all its regions, from the Coastal Plain to the Appalachian **Plateau.**

*Temperatures are warmer near the Atlantic Ocean, in the east, and colder in the Blue Ridge Mountains, in the west, where winter winds from the north and snow are likely.*

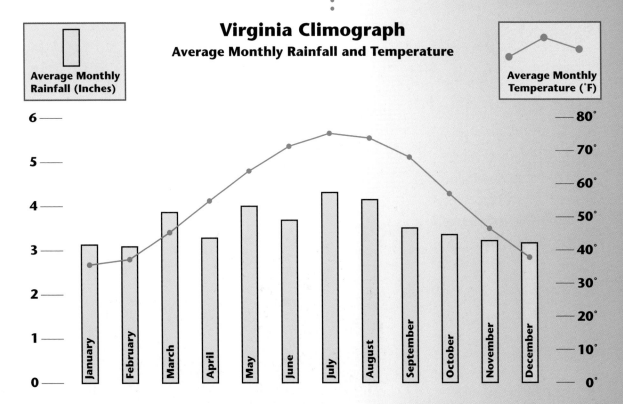

**Average Monthly Rainfall (Inches)**

# Virginia Climograph
## Average Monthly Rainfall and Temperature

**Average Monthly Temperature (°F)**

# Coastal Plain

**T**he Coastal Plain, or Tidewater, is the large area of flat land in eastern Virginia. It borders the Atlantic Ocean and includes the Chesapeake Bay. The Coastal Plain is also called the Tidewater because the lands are affected by the tides of the Atlantic Ocean. Each day, water rises and falls by two to four feet along a tidal shoreline that includes bays, rivers, and smaller bodies of water that line the Chesapeake Bay.

The Coastal Plain reaches from the Potomac River in the north to the mouth of the Chesapeake Bay in the south. To the west, it is bordered by the **fall line,** which separates the Coastal Plain from the Piedmont region.

## NATURAL RESOURCES

Water is the key **natural resource** in this part of Virginia, whether it be the ocean, a natural lake, swamps, rivers, or **canals.** Water makes **industries**

*Today, people come to the Coastal Plain to enjoy its **climate** and lifestyle.*

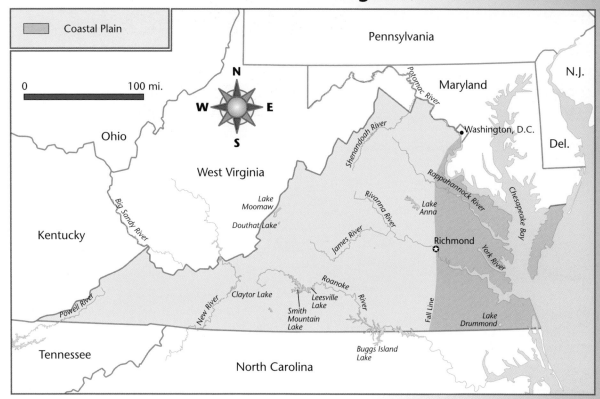

*Virginia's rivers are an important natural resource in the Coastal Plain, highlighted in the map above, as well as other regions in the state.*

such as fishing, shipping, **agriculture,** and **tourism** possible.

The biggest rivers in the Coastal Plain are the Potomac, Rappahannock, York, and James. The **sources** of these rivers are springs and rainfall that create small streams in the Piedmont, Appalachian, and Blue Ridge Mountain regions. The streams flow together to form rivers, which flow east toward sea level, where they empty into the Chesapeake Bay.

These water systems are one reason why the Coastal Plain has always been the most populated region in Virginia. Native Americans lived here first. They used the rivers for transportation. Then, in 1607, English colonists settled along the James River and built their first settlement, called Jamestown.

People have lived around the Coastal Plain's Great Dismal Swamp, in southeastern Virginia, for almost

# Virginia Population by County, 2000

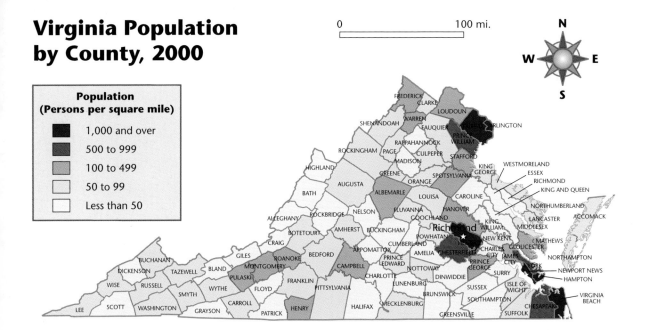

**Population (Persons per square mile)**

- 1,000 and over
- 500 to 999
- 100 to 499
- 50 to 99
- Less than 50

*The largest urban areas of Virginia are in the east. More people live in this region than elsewhere in the state.*

13,000 years. Since colonial settlement, portions of the swamp have been logged and drained. The swamp became The Great Dismal Swamp National Wildlife Refuge in 1973. It has over 109,000 acres of forested **wetlands** and a 3,100-acre natural lake, Lake Drummond, one of Virginia's two natural lakes.

The **climate** in the Coastal Plain is **temperate.** The Atlantic Ocean carries warm water to the region, in what is called the Gulf Stream. It helps make the coastal area milder than inland areas. Summers in the region are hot and **humid,** and winters are mild. This is a climate in which it is comfortable for people to live. Over half of Virginia's population lives in the Coastal Plain region.

## TRANSPORTATION

Without modern road-building skills, Virginia's settlers relied on water for transportation. The first 100 years of English settlement occurred along Coastal Plain shorelines, since the ocean made it easier to move goods and people to and from England.

## Virginia Water Facts

| | |
|---|---|
| Miles of freshwater rivers | 49,350 |
| Miles of border river | 180 |
| Number of **artificial** lakes and **reservoirs** | 248 |
| Number of natural lakes | 2 |
| Square miles of saltwater rivers, creeks, and bays | 3,315 |
| **Estuary** square miles | 2,500 |
| Atlantic Ocean coastal miles | 120 |
| Annual average rainfall | 42.8 inches |

Later, important networks of inland rivers and **canals** were used to move goods. One of these networks starts with the Elizabeth River, which flows between Norfolk and Portsmouth. This network is called the Atlantic Intracoastal Waterway (ICW), and it runs all the way to Florida. Boats of every size travel south in the fall and north in the spring along this historic waterway.

The Dismal Swamp Canal is part of the ICW. Work started on the canal in 1793, and it was completed by 1805. George Washington was part of a company that logged juniper trees, also known as Atlantic cedar, from the swamp. Cedars and **naval stores** were shipped using this network of waterways.

*The Dismal Swamp Canal is one of the oldest artificial waterways in the United States.*

# Virginia's Peninsulas

Maryland

Washington, D.C.
Arlington

N.J.

Delaware

N W E S

Potomac River

Rappahannock River

NORTHERN NECK PENINSULA

Virginia

York River

Chesapeake Bay

EASTERN SHORE PENINSULA

ATLANTIC OCEAN

Richmond

MIDDLE PENINSULA

James River

Hopewell

Appomattox River

THE PENINSULA

Jamestown

Cape Charles

Newport News

Chesapeake Bay Bridge-Tunnel

Norfolk

SOUTHSIDE PENINSULA

Virginia Beach

0          50 mi.

Virginia's Tidewater rivers divide the **mainland** into several **peninsulas.** A peninsula is a piece of land that is nearly surrounded by water. There are five peninsulas in the Tidewater.

The Eastern Shore is separated from the Virginia mainland by the Chesapeake Bay. The Eastern Shore is part of a larger peninsula that connects with Maryland and Delaware. The three states have nicknamed the peninsula Delmarva, by combining part of each state's name. The Eastern Shore is connected to mainland Virginia by the 17.6-mile Chesapeake Bay Bridge-Tunnel, pictured to the right. After it was completed in the 1960s, it was called one of the seven **engineering** wonders of the world. Before the bridge-tunnel was built, people traveled by **ferry** to get across the bay.

The other peninsulas in the Tidewater are part of Virginia's mainland. The Northern Neck peninsula is between the Potomac and Rappahannock rivers. The Middle Peninsula is between the Rappahannock and York rivers. And The Peninsula is between the York and James rivers. The lands of the Tidewater south of the James River form a peninsula called the Southside Peninsula.

The longest river in Virginia is the James River. It begins in the Appalachian Mountains and flows east for 340 miles to the Chesapeake Bay. It flows through the state capital, Richmond, at the **fall line,** and passes Virginia's first capital, Jamestown, before reaching the Chesapeake Bay.

## INDUSTRY

Virginia's major rivers end when they join the Chesapeake Bay. At that point, the rivers' mouths are several miles wide and their channels are very deep. This makes the Virginia coast perfect for the shipping **industry,** since large ships need deep water in order to come close to shore.

The body of water where the Nansemond, Elizabeth, Lafayette, and Hampton rivers join with the James River on their way to the sea is called Hampton Roads. Hampton Roads is one of the world's largest natural **harbors.** Oceangoing ships can enter the harbor because the river channels are very deep.

*__Barges__ and ships transport products up and down the James River. The river connects Richmond with international shipping piers on the Atlantic Ocean.*

Several **port** cities surround the **harbor** at Hampton Roads, and each has an important history in ship-related **industries.** Ship repair and shipbuilding are the biggest **manufacturing** sector in Virginia. Portsmouth is home to the world's biggest ship-repair yard, while the city of Norfolk is home to the world's largest naval base.

The largest privately owned shipyard on the East Coast is in Newport News. There, workers build huge aircraft carriers and repair ships from around the world. Long trains bring coal mined in Virginia's Appalachian **Plateau** to the coal piers in Newport News. More coal is **exported** from Newport News than from any other city in the United States.

*Newport News Shipbuilding designs and builds ships such as nuclear-powered aircraft carriers and submarines.*

These cities, together with Hampton, Virginia Beach, Suffolk, and Chesapeake, make up one of the fastest growing **urban** regions in the United States.

# Wild Ponies of Chincoteague

Small wild horses roam the sandy beaches and **wetlands** of Assateague Island, one of the islands in the Atlantic Ocean off the Eastern Shore coast. The Chincoteague Volunteer Fire Company holds an annual carnival and pony auction every summer. The ponies are rounded up and they swim the channel between Assateague and Chincoteague Islands. Some of the ponies are auctioned to raise money for the fire department. Thousands of people come to the islands to see the horses, made famous by the book *Misty of Chincoteague,* by Marguerite Henry.

Nine underwater tunnels and bridges connect the cities to one another. These cities form the southern end of what is called Virginia's **Urban Corridor.** Many people in the Hampton Roads area work in shipbuilding and repair, service jobs, **tourism,** and at the ports.

Hundreds of people make a living fishing the waters off the Coastal Plain. Shellfish, freshwater fish and fish from the sea are caught in Virginia's waters. Virginia is the third largest seafood producing state, bringing in over $100 million each year.

The majority of **commercial** fishing in Virginia's waters is in the Chesapeake Bay, mainly at its southern end. In Chesapeake Bay, several of Virginia's freshwater rivers mix with salt water from the Atlantic Ocean to create a unique **ecosystem** called an **estuary.** The Chesapeake

*Menhaden are one of Virginia's most valuable fish, but people do not eat them. They are ground up and made into feed for farm animals.*

Bay is the largest **estuary** in the United States.

Chesapeake Bay has been famous for its shellfish for a long time. In the early 1600s, ships had to be careful not to run aground because of the huge supply of shellfish found in the bay. Indians and colonists depended on the shellfish for food.

By the late 1800s, millions of barrels of oysters were being shipped from Chesapeake Bay to cities along the East Coast. But over-harvesting, plus disease and pollution, have reduced the oyster population by a large amount. Also, environmental changes caused by humans have reduced crab and clam harvests. Many people in the area have had to turn to other jobs to make a living, because seafood catches have fallen so much in the last few decades.

Because of the shortage of oysters, an organization called the Chesapeake Bay Foundation has been

## Chesapeake Deadrise

The workboat of Virginia fishers is unique to the Chesapeake Bay. It is called the Chesapeake deadrise and was designed to work in the shallow waters of the bay. It is used for crabbing, clamming, and fishing. Most of these boats are wooden and are painted white. Because there are now fewer oysters and fish in the area, people are turning to other occupations. Many of the wooden boats are no longer used, and wooden boat building is becoming a lost art.

working with Virginia's students to help restore oysters to the bay. Baby oysters are grown in floats in tidal waters from September until May. In the spring, the surviving oysters are placed on new oyster reefs to live.

Seafood is harvested from both the bay and the Atlantic Ocean by people living in small fishing villages on the Eastern Shore. The Eastern Shore **peninsula,** however, is mainly an **agricultural** region, with no cities and few towns. The mild **climate** and sandy soils are good for growing vegetables. Farmers raise over 60 kinds of vegetables and fruits there. Crops such as green beans, apples, and strawberries are sent to markets on the East Coast.

Most agricultural jobs on the Eastern Shore are in the poultry **industry.** Chickens are raised on farms all over the Eastern Shore. They are processed in two major plants there.

Farmers in **rural** areas in Hampton Roads produce peanuts, cotton, vegetables, and grains. Nurseries grow plants, shrubs, trees, and flowers that are shipped to markets along the East Coast.

*A student checks oysters and the water in which they live. Each month, students send reports on what they find to the Chesapeake Bay Foundation.*

*Planters Peanuts moved to Suffolk, Virginia, in 1913, where it held a logo contest. Mr. Peanut was designed by a 13-year-old boy in 1916. He won five dollars for his design.*

*Soil and weather conditions in Gloucester County are ideal for growing daffodils.*

**Agriculture** is one of the main industries on the Middle **Peninsula,** too. **Immigrants** brought daffodils to the area to remind them of their home in England. In the 1920s and 1930s especially, daffodil farms were a major industry on the Middle Peninsula. Gloucester became known as the Daffodil Capital of America. Today, the county of Gloucester is the site of a yearly daffodil festival.

The Coastal Plain's close location to Washington, D.C., and its large population make it the ideal place for government-related jobs. Many people living in the region work for the government, businesses related to the government, or **high-tech** companies.

One of the islands near the Eastern Shore peninsula is called Wallops Island. On this island, Wallops Flight Facility is part of **NASA's** Goddard Space Flight Center. It has been an important rocket launch site since 1945. The center is used to test and launch rockets and balloons as part of the space program.

Norfolk, in Hampton Roads, is the home of the world's largest naval base, called Naval Station Norfolk. The Hampton Roads area has bases for every branch of the military. More than one-third of the people living in Hampton Roads work for the United States military. Others have jobs in the high-tech computer **industry.**

Where there are people, there are services to make their lives easier. The service industry includes all kinds of services that all the people and businesses in an area use. These might include restaurants, hotels, health care services, and shops.

Service industries are concentrated in the largest cities in Virginia, mostly in the Coastal Plain region. One third of all jobs in the state are in service industries. They employ over 1.2 million people and account for the largest portion of goods and services produced in Virginia each year.

**To find out more about Virginia's gross state product, see the graph on page 7.**

Service industries also flourish where there are tourists. Many people from all over the world visit the Coastal Plain to enjoy water sports and the region's rich history. Many people visit the Historic Triangle, for example. It connects three cities: Jamestown, where the first English colonists settled; Yorktown, where the United States of America won its freedom; and Williamsburg, Virginia's second capital. Tourists come to the Coastal Plain from all over the world to visit places like these.

*Over 75 ships and 138 aircraft that are part of the U.S. Naval Fleet are in Naval Station Norfolk when they are not at sea.*

# Piedmont

**P**iedmont is the Italian word meaning *foot of mountain.* The Piedmont of Virginia is the state's largest **landform** region. It is also called the Heart of Virginia or Virginia's Midlands, because it is located in the middle of the state. The Piedmont's eastern boundary is the **fall line** and its western boundary is the Blue Ridge Mountains.

## NATURAL RESOURCES

The fall line marks the location of the last set of waterfalls on the rivers that flow eastward toward Chesapeake Bay: the James River, York River, Potomac River, and Rappahannock River. The fall line was a natural **barrier** to travel by river westward in colonial times. Boats and ships could not go past this point. This is why the cities along the fall line became important trading centers.

*Waterfalls, like the one pictured here, occur along the fall line that forms the boundary between the Coastal Plain and Piedmont regions.*

# Piedmont Region

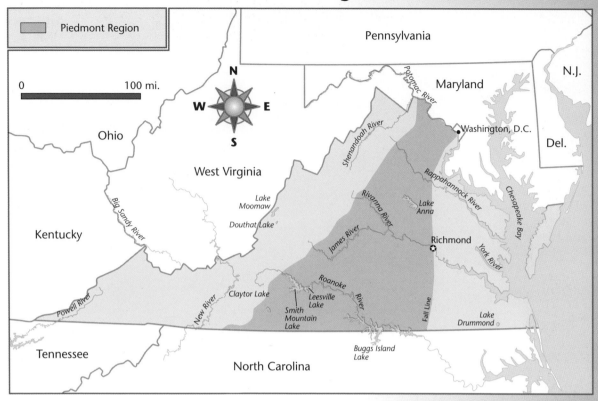

Legend: Piedmont Region

0 — 100 mi.

N W E S

Pennsylvania

N.J.

Maryland

Ohio

Washington, D.C.

Del.

West Virginia

Potomac River

Shenandoah River

Lake Moomaw

Douthat Lake

Rappahannock River

Lake Anna

Chesapeake Bay

Kentucky

Big Sandy River

Rivanna River

James River

Richmond

York River

Powell River

New River

Claytor Lake

Roanoke River

Leesville Lake

Smith Mountain Lake

Fall Line

Lake Drummond

Tennessee

North Carolina

Buggs Island Lake

Some of Virginia's largest **artificial** lakes have been built in the Piedmont region. Smith Mountain Lake, Buggs Island Lake, and Lake Gaston are **reservoirs** that provide power and water to surrounding **urban** areas. Some of the water is used for **industry** and **irrigation.** State parks and campgrounds are also on these lakes.

*The foothills and forests of the Piedmont region, west of the fall line, are home to farm communities and horse raising. They also have many outdoor activities.*

*Smith Mountain Lake is in the western part of the Piedmont. The Smith Mountain Lake Dam was completed and the lake was filled to capacity in 1966.*

*Limestone mined in the Piedmont region is crushed into lime and used to make products such as cement, iron, and glass.*

There are many **minerals** found in the Piedmont. Slate, granite, limestone, and sandstone are used for buildings and roads. In the 1700s, **iron ore** and coal were mined in the Piedmont. Coal was used for **manufacturing** and as fuel. Iron was used to make tools. Coal and iron are no longer mined in the region today.

## INDUSTRY

Piedmont rivers, because they are so fast-moving, were used in the past to create energy to power water mills. **Textile** mills were then built in towns in the region, such as Danville and Martinsville. Today these places remain important makers of textiles, clothing, and shoes. Martinsville is also known as a furniture manufacturing center.

The rivers were also used to make electric power. Today, energy from coal, gas, oil, or nuclear power is used to create electricity. Chemical plants make **artificial** fibers and plastics. The manufacture of electrical equipment and computer components are two other important **industries** in the region today.

The Piedmont region is known for its red clay soil. The region is a low **plateau** with gently rolling plains and many rivers and streams. The **climate** and soil in the southern Piedmont are ideal for growing crops such as tobacco, cotton, and corn. In the north, the soil is good for growing grasses.

The southern part of the region is famous for its tobacco crop. Tobacco is grown on only a small part of the region, south of the James River, but tobacco provides much of the farming income for the state. Tobacco, mainly grown in the Piedmont region, is the fifth biggest **agricultural** product in Virginia.

Turf grass and crops such as winter wheat are grown in the northern Piedmont. Cattle and dairy farming have passed tobacco as the top agricultural product in this

**To find out more about Virginia's gross state product, see the graph on page 7.**

*In the Piedmont region, fewer than one in every ten farms grows tobacco, but tobacco accounts for about half the value of the agricultural goods from the region.*

25

*In horse country, there are horse farms, shows, and sports. Mounted hunts and horse markets are some events that take place there.*

area. Virginia's northern Piedmont region is also known as the heart of horse country. The city of Middleburg calls itself the nation's horse and hunt capital. Virginia's most famous horse was Secretariat, the Triple Crown racing champion. In the western Piedmont, peach and apple orchards can be found in the foothills of the Blue Ridge Mountains.

### TRANSPORTATION

In colonial times, farmers living in all the areas of the Piedmont would bring their crops to the cities on the **fall line** to be shipped around the world. Cities on the fall line include Alexandria on the Potomac River, Fredericksburg on the Rappahannock River, Richmond on the James River, and Petersburg on the Appomattox River.

Alexandria is named after Captain John Alexander, who bought 6,000 acres of land in the area in 1670. By 1740, there was a public **ferry** to the opposite shore of the Potomac River. The town of Alexandria was started in 1748. George Washington helped **survey** its streets and

84 half-acre lots. Warehouses were built there for shipping tobacco and wheat.

Alexandria has a deepwater **harbor,** and it became the main **port** for **exporting** the wheat grown in the northern Piedmont. Flour wagons came into Alexandria from Piedmont and Valley settlements. Flour was then shipped to England and the West Indies. More recently, Alexandria has also become a center for research and **high-tech** businesses.

Fredericksburg was also a colonial port town, founded in the early 1700s. Piedmont farmers sent butter, hemp, cheese, flour, and tobacco to Fredericksburg. Once there, it was shipped to other colonies and England.

The state capital, Richmond, is south of Fredricksburg. Richmond has been a center for tobacco processing and shipping for 200 years. It is a center for bookmaking, **pharmaceutical** products, and several railroads. Richmond is the key city for the banking **industry** across five states. **Barges** and ships travel on the James River to Richmond. But today, interstate

*The climate and soil of the Piedmont's rolling hills are ideal for farming.*

# The Making of a Capital

Colonists tried starting a settlement at the falls of the James River as early as 1610. In 1637, they set up a trading post on land near the falls. By 1670, William Byrd II had established a trading post for furs, tobacco, and other items. It was known as Byrd's Warehouse, or Shocco. William Byrd II predicted that Richmond would become an important trading center. At that time, river bateaux, or boats for moving goods, were already bringing goods down the James River from the upland farmers.

By 1779, Richmond was made the capital of Virginia. Just as William Byrd II had predicted, Richmond became a major trading center. A **canal** was completed along the James River by 1840. Canal boats carried goods east and west. In 1836, the Richmond, Fredricksburg, and Potomac Railroad carried its first passengers out of Richmond. Its top speed was only ten miles per hour.

highways and railroads move most of the products in and out of Richmond. Richmond is Virginia's third largest city. It has many **cultural** resources, and the state government is based there.

Petersburg is south of Richmond. Like Richmond, Fredericksburg, and Alexandria, Petersburg was built as a **port** town. Ships from the Atlantic Ocean could sail to docks on the Appomattox River. Farmers traded and sold their products at markets in Petersburg. The city became a major tobacco warehouse and trade center in the 1900s. It is still a tobacco and marketing center today.

After the coming of the railroads in 1848, rail travel largely replaced river travel. Railroads helped towns such as Charlottesville grow in the 1850s. The Louisa

Railroad Company connected with the Shenandoah Valley through tunnels in the Blue Ridge Mountains. The Southern Railroad created a north-south route. The railroads brought workers, who needed hotels and restaurants, and service industries also grew.

## HISTORY

The Piedmont has a rich history. It is often referred to as the battleground of the Civil War. This is because over half the battles in the war were fought in the area between Petersburg and Washington, D.C. Richmond was the capital of the **Confederacy** and was a prime target during the war.

During the Civil War, Fredericksburg had its hardest days. It

*Peter Jefferson, Thomas Jefferson's father, was one of the first pioneers to settle the rich land west of the **fall line.** In 1737, he received land grants for a **plantation.** Later, Thomas Jefferson built a home on the plantation called Monticello, pictured below.*

# University of Virginia

The University of Virginia was founded in Charlottesville in 1819. Thomas Jefferson picked a hill two miles from the center of town and started what he called his "Academical Village." He designed its grounds and buildings, including the Rotunda, pictured here,

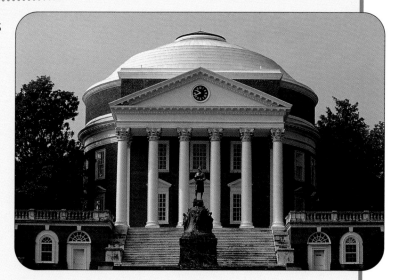

which he completed the same year he died, in 1826. Today, the University of Virginia is Charlottesville's biggest business.

was on the main road between Washington, D.C., and Richmond, Virginia. The city changed hands seven times between **Union** and **Confederate** armies. Other Civil War battles were fought near Fredericksburg. Today, Fredericksburg is a residential community that offers tourists a look at what life was like in colonial times.

Many of the places and towns in the Piedmont have become important tourist and **recreational** destinations. The tourist industry in Virginia thrives partly because of the state's rich history. Many people visit the birthplaces of the eight U.S. presidents that were born in Virginia. Since 1988, Alexandria's Old Town district has become another attraction. It has authentic buildings from the 1700s and 1800s, plus museums, restaurants, and many other services that cater to tourists.

# Blue Ridge Mountains

The Blue Ridge Mountains in Virginia start at the Potomac River in the northeast. The mountains are part of the great Appalachian mountain range, which runs along the East Coast of the United States. They were named Blue Ridge because they look misty blue in color from a distance. On a clear day, the misty-blue ridges can be seen from tall buildings in Richmond. Some of the peaks of the Blue Ridge Mountains are more than 4,000 feet above sea level. The highest mountains in Virginia are in this region. Mount Rogers, at 5,719 feet, is Virginia's highest peak.

*The Blue Ridge Mountains are the oldest mountains in North America. Some of its rock formations are more than one billion years old.*

# Virginia Topography

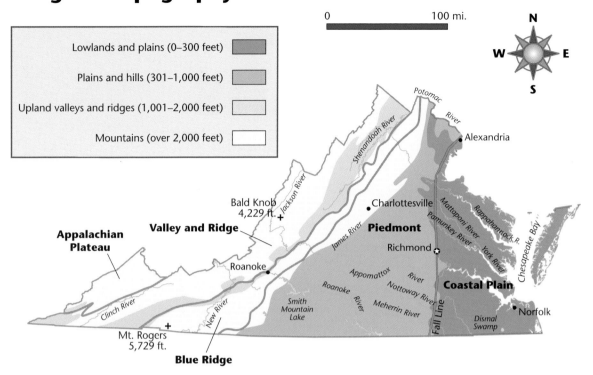

*The topography map above shows how the Blue Ridge Mountains rise at the western edge of the Piedmont region.*

## TRANSPORTATION

The Blue Ridge Mountains stopped colonists from moving west for more than 100 years. The mountain ridges were too steep and rough for wagons and horses to cross. But it was only a matter of time before the paths were cleared.

The Blue Ridge Mountains and the valley beyond them were explored in the late 1600s and again in the early 1700s. The land was thick with woods and brush. Soon after the explorations from the east, Scots-Irish settlers originally from Northern Ireland, and German settlers began traveling into Virginia. They moved down from the north, along the Shenandoah River Valley, west of the Blue Ridge Mountains.

The lands west of the Blue Ridge Mountains were mostly settled from the north. There were other, more difficult, ways to cross the Blue Ridge Mountains, but most of the 67,000 people who lived in the valley arrived from the north.

## INDUSTRY

Many more people moved to the mountains. They used the land for grazing, farms, and lumber. The chestnut tree was especially valuable. The chemicals in its bark were used to soften leather. Leather **tanneries,** which depended on the chestnut trees, were built in small towns at the foot of the mountains. As more people moved into the mountains, the land became overworked. Mountain **pastures** were **overgrazed,** and by 1900 the **natural resources** were overused.

Then, in 1915, things got even worse. The valuable chestnut tree was hit by an unknown disease. Many people depended on the chestnut tree for their jobs. When the trees died, more than half of the people moved away. The land of the Blue Ridge Mountains was worn out.

Many people moved to the small Virginia village called Big Lick, just west of the Blue Ridge Mountains. This community, which is today known as Roanoke, in the Valley and Ridge region, became the crossing for major railroads. In 1881, the Norfolk and Western Railroad

## Mining in the Blue Ridge

The earliest miners in the Blue Ridge Mountains were the **Paleo-Indians.** They looked for **quartz** to use for arrowheads. They also used **jasper** found near the base of the mountains. European settlers found **iron ore** and **manganese** ore in the mountains. Iron was mined from the colonial period until the early 1900s. Manganese was mined until the early 1960s.

combined with the Shenandoah Valley Railroad. The Roanoke Shops designed and built locomotives.

Today, the Roanoke Valley remains the center for transportation for the region. Goods and people are transported by air from the Roanoke Regional Airport. A network of fine modern highways has attracted many interstate motor freight lines. With a population of 90,000, Roanoke is the largest city in Virginia west of the Blue Ridge Mountains. It is located on Interstate 81. It is also a center for finance and trade in southwest Virginia.

*This map shows some transportation routes, such as highways, rivers, railroads, and airports, that crisscross Virginia's five regions today.*

## REUSING RESOURCES

In 1935, a large portion of the overused land in the Blue Ridge Mountain region was made into Shenandoah National Park. It holds more than 500 miles of trails, from low to high places with **panoramic** views to waterfalls in deep canyons. Deer, black bears, and wild turkeys flourish among the rich growth of an oak-hickory forest.

# Virginia Transportation

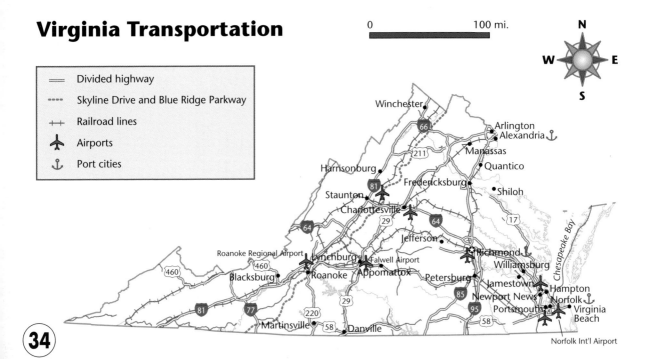

| Legend | |
| --- | --- |
| ═══ | Divided highway |
| ···· | Skyline Drive and Blue Ridge Parkway |
| ┼┼ | Railroad lines |
| ✈ | Airports |
| ⚓ | Port cities |

0        100 mi.

N W E S

Winchester
66
Arlington
Alexandria
211
Manassas
Harrisonburg
Quantico
81
Fredericksburg
Staunton
Shiloh
Charlottesville
29
64
17
64
Jefferson
Roanoke Regional Airport
Lynchburg   Falwell Airport
Richmond
460
Williamsburg
Blacksburg
Roanoke   Appomattox
Petersburg
Jamestown
460
29
85
Newport News   Hampton
Norfolk
95
Portsmouth   Virginia Beach
81
77
220
58
Martinsville   58   Danville
58
Chesapeake Bay
Norfolk Int'l Airport

# The Blue Ridge Tunnel

By the late 1800s, railroads crisscrossed the United States. However, getting tracks over the Blue Ridge Mountains was a problem. A famous French **engineer** named Claudius Crozet solved this problem. He knew how to build tunnels.

Crozet took eight years to dig and blast a way through the rocks of the mountains. His workers had to dig four tunnels. They blasted through the rock and dug by hand using picks and shovels. The longest tunnel was nearly a mile long. It was called the Blue Ridge Tunnel. Trains ran through the mountains in the Blue Ridge Tunnel for over 90 years.

Today, **tourism** has replaced **tanneries** as the key **industry** in the Blue Ridge Mountains. Small towns are dotted along the base of the mountains. Ski resorts, lodges, and campsites exist where mountain farms once were. Skyline Drive and the Blue Ridge Parkway are scenic highways with spectacular views of the beautiful landscape.

The Appalachian Trail is the most famous trail in the Blue Ridge Mountains. It is a 2,100-mile hiking trail that follows the Appalachian Mountains through fourteen states, eight national forests, and two national parks. It also crosses fifteen major rivers. Each year, about 100 hikers complete the whole trip.

# Valley and Ridge

**T**he Valley and Ridge region includes hills and long ridges with valleys between them. The Valley includes part of the Great Valley, which runs through the Appalachian Mountains, as well as other valleys separated by ridges. The ridges include part of the Allegheny Mountains in the western half. The Allegheny Mountains are part of the Appalachian Mountains which run along the East Coast of the United States. The Allegheny Mountains are a series of long mountains with narrow valleys in between.

*The valleys of the Shenandoah River, Roanoke River, New River, Clinch River, Holstein River, and Powell River are all part of the Great Valley.*

The lands of this region were once under the ocean. **Fossils** of the sea animals that lived there created limestone, which is found all through the Valley and Ridge. Limestone dissolves easily. When water dissolves underlying rocks

## Virginia's Valleys

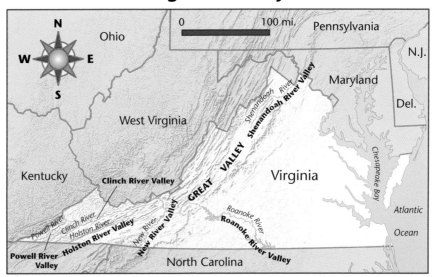

# Valley and Ridge Region

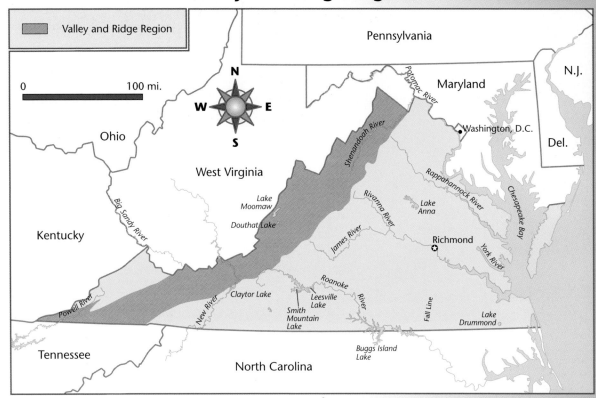

West of the Blue Ridge Mountains lies the Valley and Ridge region. It includes a series of river valleys and part of the Allegheny Mountains.

in some areas, it creates **sinkholes.** In other places, it forms underground caves. Thousands of sinkholes and caves are caused by the reaction of water with limestone in the region.

A major attraction of the Great Valley is its **climate.** Seasons vary little from year to year. Summer days are pleasantly warm, averaging 76 °F. Winter has an average

The Shenandoah Valley was the first part of the Great Valley to be settled. Between 1730 and 1760, over 67,000 settlers moved to the area. Most of them were farmers.

snowfall of 16 inches and temperatures in the mid-30s. Rarely does the temperature reach 0 °F. The valley is a **fertile** area and has an average six-month growing season fed by 35 inches of precipitation each year.

## TRANSPORTATION

Virginia's Great Valley has been an important travel route since prehistory. Early European settlers first came into the Great Valley by traveling south, along the Shenandoah River. Settlers from Pennsylvania in the north brought their families in simple carts and two-wheeled carriages. They followed an old Native American trail called the Great Warrior Path. Later, German settlers in the region moved huge wagons along the trail to transport goods to and from markets.

The trail the settlers traveled became known as the Great Wagon Road. Many

*Livestock such as poultry, pigs, beef and dairy cattle, and sheep, make the Valley and Ridge an important farming region in Virginia.*

of the towns and cities in the Great Valley today began as stops along the Great Wagon Road. Settlers built forts for protection, and these forts became small towns. One of the main stops on the Great Wagon Road was Winchester. Today, Winchester is located on Interstate 81. This Interstate follows the path of the original Great Wagon Road. Staunton and Harrisonburg were towns settled on the Great Wagon Road. Interstate 81 is a major trucking route for the eastern half of the United States.

To find out more about Virginia's transportation systems, see the map on page 34.

## INDUSTRY

Railroads were a big reason for the success of **industry** in western Virginia after the Civil War. **Agriculture** and business grew because of the railroads. Small towns grew around factories that made furniture, clothing, and other items. The railroads would take **raw materials** to these towns and bring the products the people in the towns made back to markets to the east and north.

The cities and towns in the northern Shenandoah Valley deal in agricultural supply and **manufacturing.** Wheat was the main farm product for years. But since the

### Railroad Map of Virginia, late 1800s

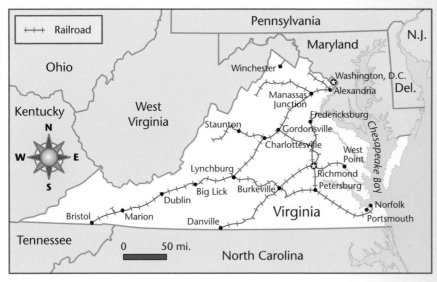

In the late 1800s, different rail lines connected western Virginia to other cities and shipping centers on the coast.

1960s, livestock has been the biggest product. Dairy and poultry products have replaced wheat as the main **agricultural** source of income.

Rockingham County in the Shenandoah Valley is among the major poultry producing counties in the United States. Rockingham County is called the Turkey Capital of the World.

Harrisonburg's location on the Great Wagon Road made the city what it is today. It became the **county seat** of Rockingham County in 1779. It remains a regional market center for farms. A good transportation network has helped attract **high-tech industries** to the area.

Rockingham County makes more money from agricultural products than any other county in the state. In fact, Rockingham County makes three times more money from agriculture than second-ranking Augusta County. It, too, is in the Shendandoah Valley. In the very north of the region, major crops such as grain and alfalfa are grown. These are sent to the livestock farms as food for the animals. Apples are also grown here.

*Winchester, Virginia's oldest city west of the Blue Ridge Mountains, is famous for its apple crop and the Apple Blossom Festival it holds every year.*

Nearer the Allegheny Mountains, the main industries are **tourism** and forestry. Public and private lands in this region provide trees for some of Virginia's paper and lumber mills. Paper and wood products are made in the mountains near Covington, a town settled in 1746. Farther south in the region, the land gets very hilly and rocky. It is used mainly for **pasture** for cattle, horses, and dairy cows.

## Higher Education

There are many colleges and schools in the Valley and Ridge region. Blacksburg, Virginia, in the New River Valley, is home to Virginia Polytechnic Institute and State University, popularly known as Virginia Tech. It started over 125 years ago as an agricultural college. Today, it is one of the state's largest universities. It has over 25,000 students. Most of the people who live in and around Blacksburg work for the university.

James Madison University and Eastern Mennonite University are in Harrisonburg, and Lexington is home to two colleges. One is Washington and Lee University, pictured here, and the other is the Virginia Military Institute. Built in 1839, the Virginia Military Institute is known as the West Point of the South. Many famous military men have graduated from the institute.

# Appalachian Plateau

The Appalachian **Plateau** is a series of gaps, ridges, and valleys that are part of a raised plateau which extends into Kentucky and Tennessee. The Clinch, Powell, and Holstein rivers carved these mountain ridges. These three rivers run southwest into the Tennessee River.

## NATURAL RESOURCES

Millions of years ago, the Appalachian Plateau region was swampy. Plants became buried under layers of sand and rock. After millions of years, this created **fossil** fuels, such as coal, natural gas, and some oil.

In 1876, large amounts of coal were found near the town of Pocahontas, in Tazewell County. In 1882, the first coal mine was opened by The Southwest Improvement Company. **Immigrants** from Hungary, Wales, Russia, Poland, Italy, Germany, and Ireland came to work in the mines.

*Coal is Virginia's most valuable mineral resource. It is used mostly to produce electricity.*

# Appalachian Plateau Region

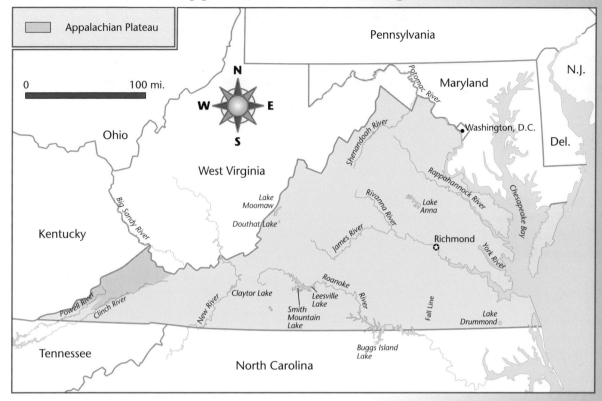

The Norfolk and Western Railroad began shipping coal to Norfolk from these coalfields in 1883. By 1910, eight rail lines were bringing coal to Virginia's **ports** to be shipped all over the world.

*The Appalachian Plateau is the smallest geographic region in Virginia. It is located in the southwest corner of the state, to the west of the other regions.*

Today, Virginia is one of the country's leading producers of this **mineral** resource. In 1997, there were over 350 coal mines in operation in just seven counties in the Appalachian Plateau. Coal is used in Virginia to produce electricity and in the **manufacture** of other products. Virginia ranks eighth in the country in coal production. Virginia's coal is exported to countries all over the world. In 1998, almost 11 million tons of coal were loaded for **export** by just one railroad.

The Appalachian Plateau region is also home to lumber and **agricultural industries.** Much of the land is used for **pasture.** Farmers raise beef cattle and sheep. Cooler temperatures are good for growing evergreen trees.

## TRANSPORTATION

Virginia's modern interstate transportation system connects the Appalachian **Plateau** to the state's other regions. Distances that took weeks to travel 200 years ago now only take hours. Virginia's transportation system moves **raw materials** to factories and finished products to markets. Trains still move goods from factories to markets, but trucks have replaced many railroads. Virginia also has twelve **commercial** airports.

To find out more about Virginia's transportation systems, see the map on page 34.

The state of Virginia has changed greatly since the first settlers made their home at Jamestown. Those settlers used the resources they found in Virginia to build new lives for themselves. Today, the people of Virginia continue to use the same resources offered by each of the state's regions. They use these resources in new and different ways, to make their lives better.

*This area of the Blue Ridge Mountains, seen from Twenty–Minute Cliff, a scenic overlook on the Blue Ridge Parkway, was probably once used as farmland.*

# Map of Virginia

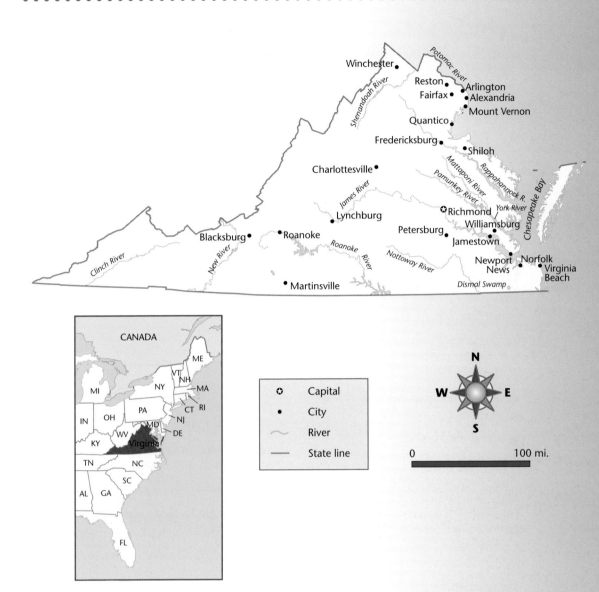

**Winchester**

**Reston** **Arlington**
**Fairfax** **Alexandria**
**Mount Vernon**
**Quantico**
**Fredericksburg** **Shiloh**
**Charlottesville**
*Shenandoah River*
*Potomac River*
*James River*
*Mattaponi River*
*Pamunkey River*
*Rappahannock R.*
*York River*
**Lynchburg**
*Chesapeake Bay*
**Richmond**
**Williamsburg**
**Blacksburg** **Roanoke** **Petersburg**
**Jamestown**
*Roanoke River*
*New River*
*Clinch River*
**Newport News** **Norfolk**
**Virginia Beach**
*Nottoway River*
*Dismal Swamp*
**Martinsville**

CANADA
ME
VT
NH
NY
MA
MI
CT RI
PA
NJ
IN OH
MD
WV DE
KY
Virginia
TN NC
SC
AL GA
FL

| Symbol | Legend |
|--------|--------|
| ✪ | Capital |
| • | City |
| ∼ | River |
| — | State line |

N
W E
S

0                100 mi.

# Glossary

**agriculture** farming

**aquifer** place with water that can be reached by wells

**artificial** made by humans

**barge** broad boat with a flat bottom used mainly in harbors and on rivers and canals

**barrier** something that blocks passage

**canal** artificial waterway or ditch

**climate** weather conditions that are usual for a certain area

**commercial** having to do with the buying and selling of goods and services

**Confederacy** eleven Southern states that withdrew from the United States in 1861–1862

**county seat** place where county government is based

**culture** ideas, skills, arts, and way of life of a certain people at a certain time. Something that has to do with culture is called cultural.

**economy** overall system of buying, selling, and using goods or services in a certain area. Things having to do with an economy are called economic.

**ecosystem** community of living things, together with the environment in which they live

**engineering** designing and manufacturing complex products

**estuary** place where salt water from the sea meets fresh water from a river

**export** good or service sent out of a country for profit

**fall line** imaginary line between the Coastal Plain and Piedmont regions along which there are waterfalls

**ferry** boat or barge that takes people or animals across water

**fertile** bearing many crops or much vegetation

**fossil** remains of prehistoric plants or animals. A fossil fuel is a fuel formed in the earth from plant or animal remains.

**harbor** protected body of water that is a place of safety for ships

**high-tech** having to do with advanced technology and computers. High-tech is short for the term high-technology.

**human resource** person who works to create goods or services

**humid** wet, damp air

**hydroelectric** electricity produced by running water

**immigrant** person who moves to another country to live

**industry** group of businesses that offer a similar product or service

**iron ore** mineral mined for the iron it contains

**irrigate** supply water to land

**jasper** smooth, red quartz stone used for making arrowheads

**landform** natural feature of the land surface

**mainland** main part of the state

**manganese** element that resembles iron but is not magnetic

**manufacturing** making goods by hand or machine

**mineral** substance formed naturally in the earth and obtained by mining

**NASA** National Air and Space Administration

**natural resource** something that is available from the land that can be useful to humans

**naval stores** substance produced from pine trees used for sealing wooden naval ships

**overgrazed** land that has been damaged by too many animals eating too much grass

**Paleo-Indian** Indian from prehistoric times

**panoramic** unbroken view

**pasture** land where animals graze

**peninsula** piece of land extending into a body of water

**pharmaceutical** having to do with medication

**physical** of or relating to nature as we see it

**plantation** farming estate cared for by laborers

**plateau** broad, flat area of high land

**port** place where ships load or unload cargo

**quartz** type of rock

**raw material** material in its natural condition

**recreation** things people do to refresh their mind and body; fun

**reservoir** place where water is collected and stored for use

**rural** of or relating to the countryside

**sinkhole** hollow ground

**source** start of a stream or river

**survey** inspect in detail

**tannery** factory where animal skins are made into leather

**temperate** not too hot or too cold

**textile** woven cloth

**tourism** industry built around people who travel for pleasure

**Union** group of states that formed the federal government during the Civil War

**urban** relating to the city

**Urban Corridor** high population area made up of several cities

**wetland** very wet, low-lying area

# More Books to Read

Harrah, Madge. *My Brother, My Enemy*. New York: Simon and Schuster Books for Young Readers, 1997.

Henry, Marguerite. *Misty of Chincoteague*. Chicago: Rand McNally & Co., 1949.

Mader, Jan. *Virginia*. Danbury, Conn.: Scholastic Library Publishing, 2003.

Marsh, Carole. *Virginia Bingo: Geography Edition*. Peachtree City, Ga.: Gallopade International, 2000.

Pollack, Pamela. *Virginia: The Old Dominion*. Milwaukee, Wis.: Gareth Stevens International, 2002.

# Index

# About the Author

Karla Smith grew up in a navy family and moved several times before settling down in Suffolk, Virginia. She has been teaching third, fourth, and fifth grade social studies since 1969. When she's not teaching, Smith enjoys exploring Virginia's waters in a sailboat.